A castle home

smelly, defending, feasting, treacherous, gloomy, crenellated, warring, fighting, jousting, ruinous, attacking, chivalrous, noisy, murderous, costly...

Dr Brian Knapp

Curriculum Visions

Dig deeper ...

books provide in-depth exploration
into classic popular topics.

... and there's more on-line

You will find multimedia resources covering a
wide range of topics at our subscription website:

www.CurriculumVisions.com

A CVP Book © Atlantic Europe Publishing 2010

Author
Brian Knapp, BSc, PhD

Editor
Gillian Gatehouse

Researcher
Lisa Magloff, MA

Designed and produced by
Atlantic Europe Publishing

Senior Designer
Adele Humphries, BA, PGCE

Printed in China by
WKT Company Ltd

A castle home – Curriculum Visions
A CIP record for this book is available from
the British Library

Paperback ISBN 978 1 86214 568 9

Picture credits
All pictures are from the Earthscape and ShutterStock
collections, except the following: (c=centre t=top
b=bottom l=left r=right) Mark Stacey 4 (top three),
29tr, 44–45; TopFoto 42–43; Wikipedia 4b, 5cl,
5bl, 22, 40–41 (background).

This product is manufactured from sustainable managed
forests. For every tree cut down at least one more is planted.

Know your castle from your castle! This is Neuschwanstein castle, one of the world's most visited 'castles'. It is in Bavaria, Germany. It is perched high on a crag of rock and almost unapproachable. It has been used for scenes in many films and inspired theme parks. But it is a fake. It was begun in 1869 and designed by a theatrical set designer, not a Norman architect. It is actually a 19th century palace. Even the name is fake, taken from an opera by the composer Wagner. Look closely and you will see that some towers look like minarets and the whole outside is filled with windows, not quite what you would have wanted in medieval times.

Contents

▼ **INTRODUCTION**
4   Summary

▼ **CASTLE DESIGN**
6   How was a castle designed?
8   Motte and tower
10   Wall
12   Bailey and ward
14   New ideas for castles
16   The king's castles

▼ **CASTLE LOCATION**
18   Where were castles built?
20   Why do you find towns and castles together?

▼ **DEFENDING THE CASTLE**
22   How to destroy an early castle
24   The siege of Rochester

▼ **CASTLE RUINS**
26   Why are castles now in ruins?
28   'Reconstructing' castle ruins

▼ **THE CASTLE HOME**
30   Getting about in a castle
32   All the comforts of home...
34   The great hall
36   Eating and entertaining
38   The garrison
40   Tournaments and jousting
42   Domesday
44   Life in Norman times

▼ **REFERENCE**
47   Glossary
48   Index

Bamburgh castle, a true castle built in Norman times along the coast of Northumberland.

Summary

A CASTLE is a nobleman's stronghold – a defended home. It wasn't a sudden invention, but an idea for protection that had been handed down over the ages.

1 The earliest 'castles' were **FORTS**. In Iron Age times (500 BC to Roman times) earth banks and ditches were built to make structures called Hill Forts and cliff castles (picture ①). The forts were for the whole tribe to retreat to.

2 The Romans built smaller forts (picture ②), but they were just for the soldiers (the garrison) who looked after each area. The walls were made from stone. Towns grew up next to many of these small forts. Later, the Romans built walls around the whole town.

3 In Saxon times, King Alfred fortified many towns. They were called burhs (picture ③).

4 The Roman Empire collapsed and many warlords fought over the lands of Europe. Eventually they became small kings, dukes and other nobles.

5 For a king or nobleman to expand his territory, it was not necessary to defeat the people in the neighbouring land. Most were just **PEASANT** farmers. All that was needed was to capture and 'remove' the neighbouring lord. The peasants would then swear allegiance to their new lord.

6 As a result, Europe's wars became power struggles between small groups of warriors. In these uncertain times, therefore, each noble needed a stronghold to help guard his safety. This is why the personal fortified house – the castle – came to be.

7 The more powerful and wealthy nobles were served by large numbers of soldiers, servants

▲ ① The earliest defences were called Hill Forts and were put up in Iron Age times.

▲ ② The Romans built forts for their soldiers.

▲ ③ The Saxons defended their towns with walls.

▲ ④ The Bayeux Tapestry shows that William knew all about castles. This part shows a

▲ ⑤ A castle began as a tower on a mound surrounded by a ditch. This is Cardiff castle.

▲ ⑥ Later on, important castles were built with rings of walls. This is the Tower of London.

▲ ⑦ Many buildings were constructed against the inside castle walls, including apartments for the nobles, GREAT HALLS and chapels. This is Windsor castle.

▶ ⑧ A castle would have foot-soldiers, archers and cavalry for attacking the enemy. In times of trouble a lord could call on KNIGHTS. To keep up their skills, knights held jousting matches and tournaments.

❽ When **NORMAN** (French) Duke William of Normandy (the Conqueror) became King William I of England after the Battle of Hastings in 1066, he knew he could not keep control of the land without help, so he gave out parcels of land to the nobles who had fought with him. It was their payment for helping, but also their job to control the land they were given. To do this, William and his Norman nobles introduced castles to Britain (picture ④). This is why most British castles were built from the 11th century.

❾ Castles were put up quickly, as a simple wooden tower (keep) on a mound of soil (motte). Digging out the soil made a surrounding ditch (moat) (picture ⑤). To make more space for soldiers (picture ⑧), servants and so on, the area of the castle was enlarged by building a loop of wall (a curtain wall) out from the motte.

❿ Then the time of the **CRUSADES** began. As a result, castle builders began to rethink how castles worked. They scrapped the idea of a keep and a single wall, and made a double wall with lots of self-contained towers set in the walls (pictures ⑥ and ⑦). All later castles had this new design.

⓫ The keep of the older castles was too small for a large number of people, so many new buildings were placed inside the inner walls, including chapels and large (great) halls, for entertaining. Castles became busy and noisy places.

⓬ Castle-building ended in the 15th century when the **TUDORS** brought peace to Britain.

Weblink: www.CurriculumVisions.com

How was a castle designed?

A castle is an important nobleman's personal home. Most British castles were built from the 11th century, when Norman (French) Duke William of Normandy (the Conqueror) became King William I of England after the Battle of Hastings in 1066. Castle-building ended in the 15th century (the end of the age of the Wars of the Roses, just before Tudor times).

Castles had many common features (picture ①). The earliest castles needed to be put up quickly and they had just a single tower (**KEEP**) on a mound (**MOTTE**). Over the centuries they grew by adding an enclosing wall (**CURTAIN WALL**). Warkworth castle, Northumberland (shown on this page), is of this design. Castles founded in later times (such as Caerphilly, page 14) did not have a keep on a mound but instead had 'walls within walls'.

Gatehouse with **PORTCULLIS** and **DRAWBRIDGE**

Outer **BAILEY** (or outer ward)

Towers

MOAT

Curtain wall

Lord's living quarters and chapel

Well

Inner **BAILEY** (or inner ward)

Remains of workshops, cookhouse, stables etc.

POSTERN tower

Crenellated (embattled) top of wall (also called battlements)

Keep

Sloping (battered) wall base to keep siege engines away. Arrow firing slits in walls

Watchtower

Motte

▲▶ ① Key to the ruins. (Only features common to most castles are indicated.)

Motte and tower

The earliest and simplest kind of castle was a tower on a mound, or motte, and a long, usually horseshoe-shaped wall (curtain wall) that looped out and back from the tower to protect a large open space called a BAILEY. As a result, the early castles are called motte and bailey castles.

▶ ① The motte and keep at Cardiff castle. This is a very simple design of keep, and archers could not see along all of the walls to keep off attackers.

The tower or keep

The simplest thing to build is a stronghold – a simple house strengthened to protect it from attackers. If this building stands on its own it is called a tower house.

It needs to have thick walls so it cannot be battered down. It should not have an entrance at ground level, for that would make it too easy to enter. It should only have slits for windows so that people inside could not be shot. It should have a lead roof so that fire arrows would do no harm.

Small tower homes like this were quite common in later centuries. But they were not suitable for powerful lords nor a king.

Tower and motte

In the Iron Age people dug ditches around the top of a hill to stop attackers charging up. It worked. Digging the ditch created lots of soil that Iron Age people used to make tall earth walls. That made it even harder to attack.

The same idea can be seen in the castle. People lived in the tower, but it would be harder to attack if it were on a mound and surrounded by a ditch. The ditch is called a **MOAT**. It would be even harder if the moat were filled with water (picture ①).

The ditch is such an important idea that you find it around the motte and, when the curtain wall was built, a moat was built around that, too.

The keep was, in a way, like a block of apartments. Keeps are now just part of a castle because, as time went by, a keep on its own was not strong enough to stand up to attack and, in addition, its quarters were cramped. So, when you think about a keep, imagine it without any of the surrounding walls, at a time when there was just a keep on a motte.

Keeps come in all shapes and sizes, depending on the designer at the time. The earliest British keeps were square, but later ones were often round.

The keep often had towers at each corner, which rose above the main building to act as watchtowers (pictures ② and ③). They also contained spiral staircases and were used to get between floors within the keep.

Living quarters

The lowest floor of the keep contained store rooms and a **CRYPT**. The only way down to this floor was via a spiral staircase from the first floor (this was the part which, in later years became used as a dungeon).

The entrance was not at ground level, but on the first floor (page 31). The outside stairs were separated from the keep by a drawbridge. This was part of the defence.

▲ ② The tower at Warkworth was rebuilt in the 14th century and has a more complicated design than the Cardiff keep. This kind of tower had no blind spots and archers could fire along all of the walls.

▲ ③ If the worst came to the worst, the defenders might try to escape. For this purpose there was often a small door in the keep and also in the curtain wall. It was called the **POSTERN**.

The first floor was used by the castle's garrison for sleeping and eating. They could also defend the main door from there.

The second floor of the keep contained the main hall. Usually there was just a large single hall for living and eating, with an area curtained off for the lord's family to sleep in. It was a kind of open-plan living. The cooking was done in the hall and also in the bailey. Sometimes an extra floor was added for chambers used by the nobleman and his family. This floor might also have had a chapel.

Wall

The wall was the main defensive structure of the castle. It had to be high and very thick.

A very basic castle is a tower on a mound. But it was not ideal. For instance, the cavalry who helped to protect the castle had nowhere for their horses (picture ①). Castles also had big staffs, and blacksmiths, saddlers and other trades needed a place to do their work. This is why the curtain wall was built.

Towers

The wall was crenellated, but it was further protected with towers (pictures ②, ③, ④ and ⑤). The towers jutted out beyond the line of the wall. Archery slits in these towers allowed defenders to shoot along the line of the wall – an important requirement if a siege engine or scaling ladders were being used by attackers.

Gatehouse

The double gate was made of massive wooden beams reinforced by iron. Nevertheless, it was still

▶ ① **The cavalry were sent out to attack any advancing army, but horses and men needed to be housed somewhere. This was one of the reasons for building a wall to protect the bailey. (Note that most cavalry were not knights, but simple soldiers.)**

the weakest part of the whole arrangement and could be attacked with a battering ram. The walls were so thick that a battering ram was useless against them (see page 23). To protect the gate, great towers were built around it (picture ⑤). The gate was further protected with a **DRAWBRIDGE** over the moat and iron grills (**PORTCULLISES**) that could be lowered to bar the way through the gatehouse (picture ⑥). Some castles had several portcullises (picture ⑦).

▲ ② **The number of towers depended on the size of the wall. An attacker must come under fire from two towers at the same time, so they could not be too far apart.**

▲ ④ A walkway and access stairs allowed archers to run to their positions when the castle was attacked.

▲ ③ Despite all of the protection, the walls might still be attacked. To make this more difficult, archers were positioned on the top of the walls. They were given protection from attackers by upstanding wall sections (merlons), while they could shoot out from the lowered sections (crenels). The protection sections were usually twice as long as the firing sections. The up and down pattern, which we sometimes call battlements, is called CRENELLATION. A noble had to apply to the king for permission to build like this. It was called a licence to crenellate.

▼ ⑤ The massive gatehouse of Harlech castle. There would also have been a drawbridge during the time it was in use.

▼ ⑥ If the portcullis was attacked, archers would rush down the towers and fire from ground level through the slits you can see here. Others would stand in the room above and pour boiling water through holes in the roof. These were called 'murder holes'.

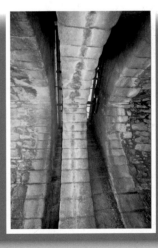

▲ ⑦ Looking up to see the place where two portcullises used to drop.

Bailey and ward

The space inside the wall was usually called the BAILEY. In some later castles it was called the WARD. It might seem a big empty space today, but in medieval times there were buildings lining all the walls. As a result the cavalry had to use the space outside the gates for jousting and other exercises.

Staff and garrison

There were two kinds of people who lived in the castle with the lord. There were the domestic staff who waited on the lord, cooked food, looked after the surrounding estate, collected taxes and so on, and then there was the garrison, made up of foot soldiers (men-at-arms) and cavalry.

Castles were not home to thousands of armed men. No one could afford the cost. A few battles were fought between thousands, but these armies were made up by taking a few dozen from the garrison in each castle along the marching route and commanding peasants on each estate to

Stables

leave their fields and join the army. Imagine the cavalry troop in the Wild West forts and you get the idea of the normal scale of things in a medieval castle.

Most castles had a few tens of cavalry and perhaps a few more men-at-arms. But all the same, they had to be housed somewhere, as did their horses. In this picture the whole left-hand side of the bailey was used for stables, smithy and other trades.

Great hall

In early days the lord and lady lived in the keep, but the rooms were rather small. So, over the centuries, many nobles had a second hall built in the bailey. On one side they had their own bedrooms and a chapel and on the other side a kitchen.

In picture ① these buildings occupied all the right hand side of the bailey, although only the entrance tower remains.

▼ ① **A view over the castle bailey.**

Gatehouse

Chapel

Great hall

Bailey

New ideas for castles

The early castles were designed around a single tower on a mound because this was quick and easy to build and relatively cheap. Over the centuries, loops of walls were added to make more room. But during the 13th century, castles were redesigned from the ground up.

The weakness of the early castles were the walls. It was all too easy to undermine a single wall. So the newer designs of castle had a double ring of walls (pictures ①, ② and ③). These new castles had no central tower (keep) at all. Instead, the main buildings were placed against the inner wall. The outer towers were made like a keep, so each could be independently defended. They were almost impossible to conquer by force.

Crenellations (battlements)

▼ ① **The narrow outer ward (space between the two sets of walls) was a death trap for attackers.**

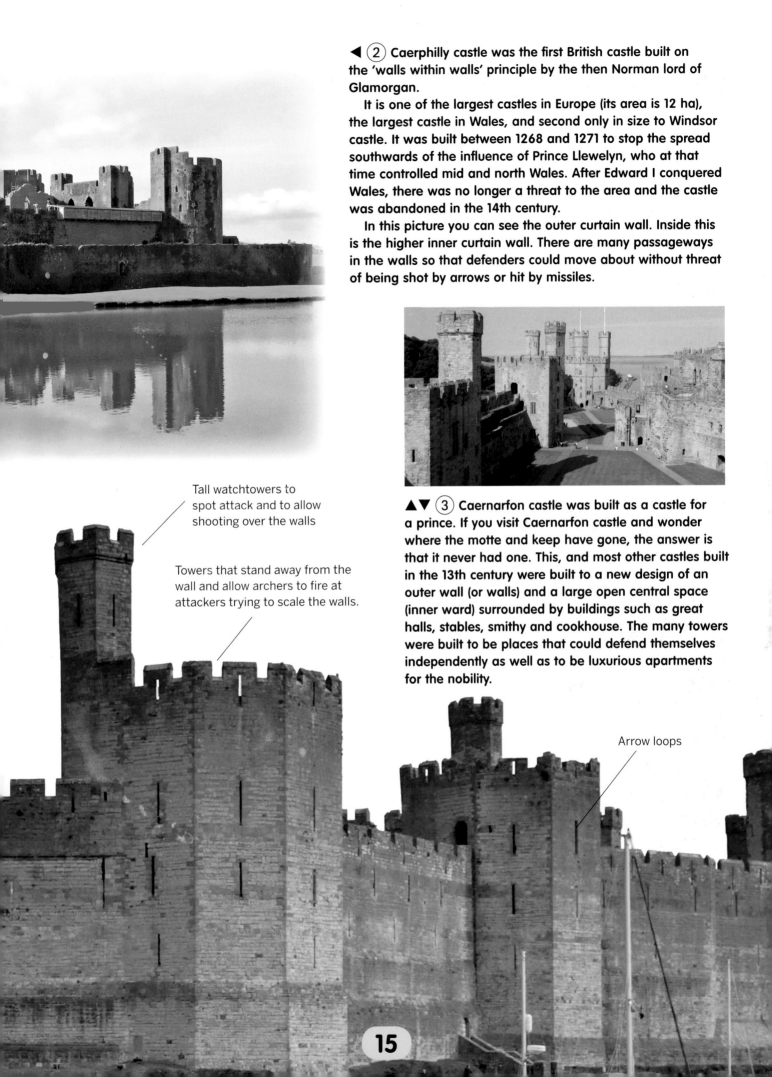

② Caerphilly castle was the first British castle built on the 'walls within walls' principle by the then Norman lord of Glamorgan.

It is one of the largest castles in Europe (its area is 12 ha), the largest castle in Wales, and second only in size to Windsor castle. It was built between 1268 and 1271 to stop the spread southwards of the influence of Prince Llewelyn, who at that time controlled mid and north Wales. After Edward I conquered Wales, there was no longer a threat to the area and the castle was abandoned in the 14th century.

In this picture you can see the outer curtain wall. Inside this is the higher inner curtain wall. There are many passageways in the walls so that defenders could move about without threat of being shot by arrows or hit by missiles.

▲▼ ③ Caernarfon castle was built as a castle for a prince. If you visit Caernarfon castle and wonder where the motte and keep have gone, the answer is that it never had one. This, and most other castles built in the 13th century were built to a new design of an outer wall (or walls) and a large open central space (inner ward) surrounded by buildings such as great halls, stables, smithy and cookhouse. The many towers were built to be places that could defend themselves independently as well as to be luxurious apartments for the nobility.

Tall watchtowers to spot attack and to allow shooting over the walls

Towers that stand away from the wall and allow archers to fire at attackers trying to scale the walls.

Arrow loops

The king's castles

When the king visited other parts of the country, he would stay with one of the great nobles in their castle. Such castles were often almost as grand as the royal castles. However, the king also had his own royal castles. The most important royal castle was the Tower of London. The Royal 'holiday home' was Windsor castle. The king could go between these along the River Thames.

The Tower of London

Because London was the normal residence of the king, the Tower of London was kept up to date with the latest fashions in castle-building. The Tower was one of the first castles to be built, so it was originally just a keep, known as the White Tower (picture ①), on a motte. But as it was so important, its defences could not be allowed to go out of fashion and so it was rebuilt time after time. This is why it is surrounded by a double wall (picture ②) that would normally only be found in later castles. Windsor (picture ③) did not need this level of protection and so it remained with a single wall. The central keep of the Tower of London was one of the first keeps to be built of stone and was begun in 1078, just twelve years after the Norman conquest of England.

▶ ① The White Tower.

William ordered the Tower to be built of white limestone brought from his native city of Caen in Normandy. The tower was finished in 1087.

In 1240 Henry III had the tower whitewashed which is how it became known as the White Tower. Its walls are up to 5m thick and rise 27m from the ground. (The building that protected the entrance stairs has long been removed, so can no longer be seen).

▲ ② **The Tower is surrounded by a double curtain wall with towers on all but the river side.**

▲▶ ③ **Windsor castle is Britain's biggest castle and is on a spur of high land commanding the route along the River Thames. It has a keep with two baileys and only one curtain wall. The royal chapel and other public areas are on the left, the royal apartments are on the right. It was used as a royal 'holiday-home'.**

Where were castles built?

A castle had a job to do: it had to guard an important place, such as a river valley or a route along a coast. You can see this by looking again at Warkworth.

Warkworth castle was built in the narrow neck of a river loop so that the natural advantages of the land were used to the full (picture ②). The loop (meander) of the river acts as a natural moat and the castle simply has to defend the land by the neck. It is also built on naturally high ground. Adding the motte makes this ground even higher.

The river has many loops, but the one chosen was close to the sea. This means the castle garrison could defend against invaders coming by ship (picture ①). The castle is also well sited to defend against any army marching along the coast. You would not want to march past this castle and then find the garrison coming out and attacking you from the rear.

▼ ① **If you invaded from the sea and wanted to go inland along the river, you would have come under withering arrow fire from the castle.**

▶ ② **This view (right) shows the castle, the town, the great loop of the river, the moat, the main road and the closeness to the coast. Notice the town grew inside the bend, not out beyond the moat: the space beyond the moat needed to be kept clear so that attackers could be spotted. In medieval times there would have been no trees on the river banks for a similar reason. They have all grown since.**

Why do you find towns and castles together?

Castles are rarely found on their own. Usually a castle and town grew up together (pictures ①️ and ②️). For most of the time the castle was not needed for warfare. But inside it lived the wealthiest person in the region (made so mainly by the taxes he collected from everyone else). He had a garrison, horses and servants, all of whom needed food, clothes and more. So he was an important employer. When there was a threat of attack, it was easy for the townsfolk to rush inside the castle gates. This was important, for an attacking army might show no mercy to people living along the route of their march.

▼ ①️ **In the view below you can see the castle on the left and the town occupying the loop in the river. A bridge carries the coastal road across the river. You can't cross the river any closer to the sea because the land is marshy. Geographers call it the lowest bridging point of the river.**

Notice how the town houses lining the road from bridge to castle have very long 'gardens'. These are, in fact, medieval smallholdings (known as BURGAGE PLOTS) because townspeople had to grow much of their own food. These plots are very rare.

◀ ② What the castle and village or town might have looked like in medieval times.

How to destroy an early castle

Castle life was a mixture of feasts, routine and occasionally fear when an attack took place. But there were rules to attack and surrender.

The main job of the castle was to defend the lord from attack, although in Britain it was often the last retreat of a lord who had rebelled against the king. In Europe, war in the Middle Ages tended to move from castle to castle. Once a castle was taken, the armies would move on to the next castle. If a castle could hold out, the enemy army would be bogged down and unable to proceed.

There were many ways to attack a castle, but it was not easy to attack it head on, especially if it had a large garrison. So, with large castles the most common tactic was a **SIEGE**. The enemy would surround a castle and not allow food in or people out.

Lords and ladies often fled before the siege. This was preferable to being caught and ransomed, or being killed. If you were the lord and outside the castle, you could raise troops or seek friendly help. You probably left your right-hand man, called the constable,

▲ ① **Attackers might use all kinds of towers to allow their men to get to the top of the walls. This tower is called a belfry.**

and his garrison to the sordid task of defending the castle and you tried not to get bottled up in the castle yourself. The postern gate was very useful for escaping.

A siege was very unpleasant. As food ran low, everyone was put on rations. Women and children were sometimes forced out of the castle and left defenceless, since they were no help in defending it and ate valuable rations.

The constable usually had an arrangement with the lord as to what to do when a siege began. The attackers and defenders knew the rules of the game and mostly they played by them. If the constable could see there was no chance of winning, he would surrender and come out with colours flying and suffer no disgrace. Agreed surrender had other advantages, such as leaving the castle undamaged. Things only got nasty if the defenders decided to stay and defend. Then the attackers would spare no one. In 1224, for example, Bedford castle was besieged by King Henry III and it held out for eight weeks. When it was finally taken, the constable and all the senior men in the garrison were hung.

If you had to attack, rather than set a siege, you could use various methods.

Fire

Fire was the best way to attack the 11th and 12th century motte and bailey castles since the tower and protecting fence were made entirely of wood. The fire might be started by building a bonfire against the outer wooden fence (palisade) or, more usually, by archers shooting fire-arrows (arrows with rags soaked in pitch and tar) into the castle. By the late part of the 12th century most castles were made of stone, but firing into the bailey might still set the lord's buildings alight.

Battering ram

The thick stone walls of the stone castles were difficult for men to knock down. The battering ram was rarely used on walls, but it could be useful on the gatehouse (picture ②). The men working the battering ram protected themselves from arrows and stones with a mobile roof.

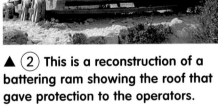

▲ ② **This is a reconstruction of a battering ram showing the roof that gave protection to the operators.**

Scaling ladders

Ladders were used to reach the top of the walls, but defenders would try to push the ladders away, or fire down on those climbing up.

Siege tower (also known as a belfry)

This was a large roofed wooden tower on wheels that could be pushed up to the castle walls (picture ①). It was the same kind of idea as the protection given to the battering ram. The sides were made from animal hides, soaked in water so they would not catch light if fire-arrows were aimed at them. To prevent the use of the siege tower, the bottoms of castle walls were often splayed out (battered).

Siege engines

Many kinds of catapults were made. A common kind was called a trebuchet. Catapults were used to throw stones, fireballs and even plague victims, over the walls. A trebuchet was powered by a massive counterweight on one end of an arm, and a sling on the other end. The ballista worked similar to a crossbow, but instead of a flexible bow, it used two stiff arms powered by twisted ropes. The ballista was used to hurl stones and also bolts or darts. (This is where we get the word "ballistic.")

Undermining

Attackers could dig a tunnel below the castle walls. They would then set fire to the tunnel woodwork, causing the walls to collapse. It was one of the most common ways to attack as few men were lost in the mining.

Treachery

Someone inside the castle would be paid to open the gates late at night and let an enemy force inside for a surprise attack.

The siege of Rochester

◀▼ ① Rochester consisted of a curtain wall and a keep.

The years after the conquest by the Normans were not calm and quiet. Battles for the throne meant almost constant warfare. By 1160 it had become clear that the keep was not as secure as had been hoped.

If you remember, a keep has high walls – good for using as defence, but they will readily collapse if the foundations are not secure.

Because the keeps at this time were mainly square they also had defensive blind spots – places where archers could not see the attackers to fight them. It was for these reasons that keeps changed from being square to having many sides, being round, or having round towers added to them (see the one in this picture). Round towers also stood up better to battering rams. You can see how important this was through the siege of Rochester (pictures ① and ②).

After Magna Carter

You may know that, at the beginning of the 13th century, the king was John 1 (reigned 1199–1216). He became hated by the powerful barons. Eventually, they used their might to force John to sign a 'bill of rights' at Runnemede by the Thames near Windsor castle, in 1215. The bill was called Magna Carta.

But John did not really want to agree to this, and he wrote to the Pope asking him to declare it unlawful. It was at this point that the barons staged a revolt. It was civil war.

A group of barons rushed to the Kentish port of Rochester on the River Medway and seized control of the castle. On 11th October King John was travelling from Dover to London and found his route blocked by the defenders in the castle. John was determined to take the castle by force. The result was one of the biggest and most spectacular sieges in English history.

The rebels were expecting reinforcements from London but John sent fire ships to burn the bridge over the River Medway and so stop them arriving. Five siege engines were then erected against the castle walls and a tunnel dug to undermine the outside (curtain) wall. By early November the king's men had reached the bailey and then began tunnelling under the keep. The tunnel roof was supported by wooden props, which were then set alight using the fat from 40 pigs.

The burnt timbers gave way, the tunnel collapsed and the whole corner of the keep fell down. However, the keep had a dividing wall (called a cross wall) inside it, so although half of the keep was damaged, the defenders were able to keep the king at bay using the remainder of the keep. A few rebels were allowed to surrender and leave the castle but, on John's orders, had their hands and feet cut off.

The keep held out, even though hunger meant that the men inside had to eat their own horses.

The castle was finally taken on 30th November by starvation and not by force. The remainder of the rebel barons were taken away and imprisoned at various royal-held castles. The siege against just 100 rebels cost over a thousand pounds a day (millions in today's money). But the lesson for any would-be defender was that better castle designs were needed. This was one reason the walls within walls castle came into being (page 14).

▼ (2) **Tunnelling undermined one of the square towers like this. That is why it was rebuilt as a round tower – see picture opposite.**

Why are castles now in ruins?

Castles are some of the most expensive buildings ever made. They were expensive to build (needing huge amounts of materials and a large number of workers), and they were expensive to run (needing not just a garrison, but people to cook, look after horses, wait on table, and so on). By the end of the Middle Ages, they were an expensive folly as well as an uncomfortable home.

Just like any house, castles needed to be maintained, or the roof would leak, the walls would lose their cement and so on. So castles had to pay their way, that is it had to be so vital to have a castle that all of the costs were worth it.

By Tudor times, nobles had much less need to protect themselves from attack – unless they rebelled against the king or queen. There were also better and more comfortable ways of living. So nobles built themselves stately homes and let their castles fall to wrack and ruin (picture ③).

Castles are also made of good stone, or at least the outer skins of castle walls are. This is material that could be put to many other uses, so once a castle was abandoned, people often stole the stone to make new houses.

Some lords found themselves penniless and so they actually sold off their own castles, selling, for example, the lead off the roof (picture ②).

▼ ① **The walls of this castle were probably pulled down by parliamentary forces in the 17th century.**

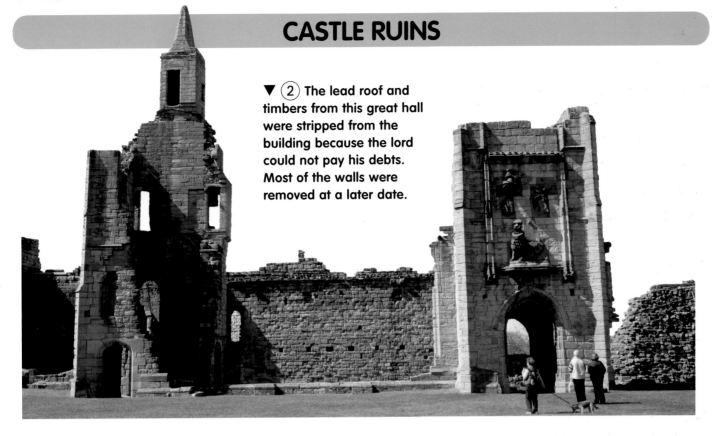

▼ ② The lead roof and timbers from this great hall were stripped from the building because the lord could not pay his debts. Most of the walls were removed at a later date.

In the 17th century, Britain was at war with itself. Those supporting the king often used castles as a base and those supporting parliament used cannon to dislodge them. This caused walls to be broken down.

To make sure they could not be used again, parliamentary forces often pulled down the walls and took away the gates (picture ①).

So, as you can see, there were many reasons for castles becoming ruins. Only the wealthiest families kept their castles as going concerns and that is why so few survive today.

▼ ③ The tower on this castle is toppling into the moat because no one wanted to pay for it to be rebuilt.

Weblink: www.CurriculumVisions.com

'Reconstructing' castle ruins

When you visit a castle, it is often in ruins. So how can you imagine what was once there?

Let's start with the interior of Rochester castle keep in picture ①. First we can see that there are some arches and pillars. One on the left is very grand and must have therefore been the entrance to the great hall. There are also socket holes at two levels in the walls. Imagine a floor/ceiling in those places. When you do this you will see that two sets of openings on the right look out into the same great hall, so one set is a gallery. A well shaft opens out into the great hall, too.

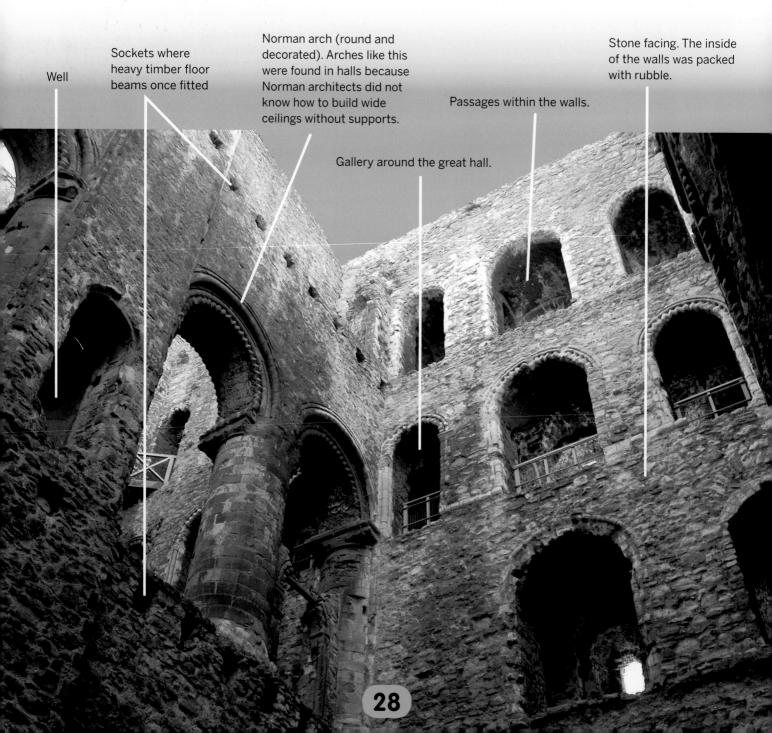

Well

Sockets where heavy timber floor beams once fitted

Norman arch (round and decorated). Arches like this were found in halls because Norman architects did not know how to build wide ceilings without supports.

Gallery around the great hall.

Passages within the walls.

Stone facing. The inside of the walls was packed with rubble.

▲ ② **Historical artists can attempt to reconstruct what life might have been like.**

So just from a brief glance we can start to imagine it as it was. Now, if we go to a place where the beams are still intact (such as Portchester, picture ② left), we can see just what the roof beams looked like.

Now we can put these things together and make a reconstruction of a typical great hall in its earliest days. (This is not meant to be a reconstruction of Portchester, but a generalised reconstruction.) Notice the wall hangings and a section curtained off for the use of the keep owner. We have now put people, furniture and a central fire all in place. In later times, chimneys were fitted and the fire moved to the side of the hall (see page 35).

▶ ③ **If you visit a ruined castle, you can think of what it might have been like by drawing frameworks in your mind's-eye, or taking a photograph and drawing frames on, as has been done here.**

▼ ④ **The holes in the walls (left) are where the massive floor timbers were fitted. Floorboards were placed on top of them. You can see this in the reconstruction (below right).**

Getting about in a castle

Castle walls were so thick they had passageways and stairs built inside them.

A castle was meant to keep those who lived in it safe from attack. This is why castles had thick stone walls. In fact, the walls were not just thick, they were very, very thick – usually several metres.

The walls were thick enough to have stairs and corridors built inside them (picture ①). This made it more comfortable to get about in winter and very much safer if the castle was being attacked.

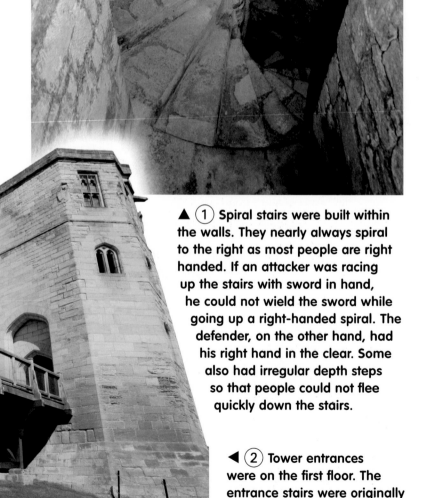

▲ ① Spiral stairs were built within the walls. They nearly always spiral to the right as most people are right handed. If an attacker was racing up the stairs with sword in hand, he could not wield the sword while going up a right-handed spiral. The defender, on the other hand, had his right hand in the clear. Some also had irregular depth steps so that people could not flee quickly down the stairs.

◄ ② Tower entrances were on the first floor. The entrance stairs were originally protected by a stone gallery and inside the door may have been a portcullis.

Early towers really were needed for defence and so had only tiny window slits. Later towers were built with more comfort in mind, and the sides of the tower, especially facing the bailey, often had larger windows, letting more light into the stairs and rooms.

Upstairs, downstairs

Castle keeps were built with the entrance on the first floor (picture ②). There was no entrance on the ground floor. This meant that an attacker had to climb the stairs to the front entrance, and so was more easily repelled. The higher up you went, the safer it was – at least for a while – and so the rooms used by the lord and lady were on the first and second floors. In later towers the bedrooms were on higher floors still.

The entrance to the great hall, where the lord held court and met guests was reached by a grand staircase (picture ③).

The stairs down to where the food and drink were kept – buttery, pantry, wine and beer cellars – were not used by the lord and so were of lower quality (picture ④). You can see the difference in these pictures.

▲ ③ **Stairs from the entrance to the great hall.**

◀ ④ **Stairs down to the cellars.**

All the comforts of home...

In the earliest days of castles, everyone lived in a keep made of a single room. But as towers were rebuilt, they became larger and had more rooms in them.

In the early days the hearth for the room was in the centre and hot, smoky air had to find its own way out of the tower. Then fireplaces were invented and the grandest towers built or rebuilt in the 14th century had fireplaces and chimneys set inside the walls, and even chimney pots on the roof. Kitchens (pictures ①, ②, ③ and ④) were then built into the lower floors of the tower.

In the earliest castles, the lord and lady slept in an area of the great hall that was just curtained off from where everyone else slept. Everyone 'did their business' on the floor or outside. By the 14th century the lord and lady, and some of the high officials, each had their own sitting room, bedroom and loo (**GARDEROBE**) (pictures ⑤ and ⑥) – in fact, they had en-suite living.

Kitchen

▲ ① Looking up the kitchen chimney shows fine stonework.

▲ ② The kitchen had a water supply and drains.

◀ ③ A cauldron was placed here to stay hot.

◀ ④ Two massive fireplaces were needed to cook for the castle staff. Great fires would have been fitted with cauldrons for the stew (potage) most people ate, and the roasting spits for the game the nobility ate.

Long-drop toilet (garderobe)

Garderobe (toilet) tower with ventilation windows

Waste falls down tower chute

Outflow

▲▶ ⑤ Garderobes were either inside the keep, in a separate tower, or fitted to the outside of the tower. The whole of this garderobe was within its own tower. Garderobes were set en-suite off the lord's bedchamber at the end of a corridor inside the walls. There were little windows to give ventilation and light. You might have sat on a wooden seat (missing in this picture) placed over a stone-lined hole. What you did fell down a chute within the walls and shot out along a sloping exit hole on the outside of the walls.

In case you were wondering, centre right is what an attacker might see when looking up the chute to fire an arrow on an unsuspecting loo user. Many chutes had a dog's leg shape to prevent such direct fire. Top right is a view of the whole loo room, which is pretty commodious.

▶ ⑥ The garderobe at Peveril castle, Derbyshire is the small projection from the castle wall. It has a tiny window. Waste fell down into a cess pit at the foot of the wall. It was designed so that no attacker could shoot up into the garderobe – with possibly unpleasant consequences for the user!

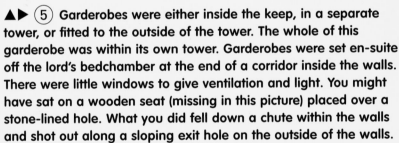

The great hall

The hall (which nowadays tends to be called the great hall) was the centre of life in the castle. This is where the lord and lady presided over public life in the castle.

The hall was the most important room in the castle (pictures ① and ②). In early tower castles it was the main room on the first floor of the keep. In later castles it was a large room built against an inner castle wall. In both cases, the hall was where the castle owner and family conducted business.

Someone from our world, which is obsessed with cleanliness, might find the hall pretty repulsive. The floor was usually timber, with rushes spread over it. It was common for people to relieve themselves without leaving the room. When people had finished their food, they simply tipped the remains, such as bone, on the floor. Mixing

herbs with the rushes helped keep down the smell until the rushes were swept away and new ones laid (which was not very often).

▼ ① A great hall as it might have been in the 15th century. Notice that the hall is taller than it is wide. The tables are planks resting on trestles (although the benches are of joinery). Many halls had a minstrel gallery where players would entertain while the diners ate. A large window faced out on to the bailey. This picture looks towards the lord's table. Normally, the passageway next to this table would lead to the lord's private apartments. Most great halls also had a large fireplace as this was the main living room of the castle. The tables would be cleared away and some of the servants would sleep on the floor at night. There were tapestries on the walls. The floor in this picture is cleaner than it would have been in the 15th century.

▲ ② A great hall with painted wall decoration and a large fireplace. (The furniture is more recent.)

It was dark inside the great hall of a Norman keep because it was not a good idea to have large windows in case of attack. Window glass was difficult to make, and large open windows simply made a cold room colder still in winter. The windows were closed over with shutters. As a result, some kind of lighting was needed all the time. Animal fat (tallow) was widely used as it is a concentrated source of energy. An alternative was oil lamps hung from a chandelier. Candles were used and rush lights were sometimes placed in brackets on the walls.

More light came from the fire. In the earliest castles, the fire was in the middle of the room, for there were no chimneys. There might not be an opening in the roof to let the smoke out either, although some people used a vent with louvred sides so the smoke could get out, but the rain could not get in. Even when the main rooms were on the first floor, they needed heating, so fires had to be placed on stone slabs on the timber floors.

When there is simply a single room used for everything, you have to find some way of dividing it up. The castle owner would most likely sit to eat on a raised platform at one end, while everyone else would sit on benches on the floor. At night the benches would be cleared way and a curtain drawn across the raised area. The castle owner would then sleep with a small amount of privacy. Everyone else slept on the main floor. Beds were not common except for the wealthiest nobles.

Hall improvements

By the 13th and 14th centuries, castles were modified to have fireplaces against the walls and proper chimneys were also fitted. By the 13th century great halls built against curtain walls often had large windows looking out onto the bailey. By the 14th century most windows were glazed.

Life also become a little more private for the owner, the constable and other notables, who had their own living apartments built next to the hall.

The more wealthy owners had a great chamber, a bedroom where they slept separately from the castle staff. There might also be another for the constable and any special guests.

35

Eating and entertaining

The main activity of a nobleman's day was to gorge himself silly on huge amounts of food.

Dining arrangements

Most people ate with their knives and a wooden spoon. Forks had not been invented. Most plates (platters) were of wood, as were many goblets. Pewter goblets were restricted to the very wealthy. When finished they might be wiped clean, but the idea of washing had not occurred to most people as they did not know that germs existed.

Rich people used 'disposable' platters, made of a square of hard, stale bread. These were called trenchers, and given as alms (gifts) to the poor after the meal.

Meals for the lord and high officials

Eating well was all about eating in the right order. For example, it was thought that you should eat lighter foods first and heavier foods afterwards. In many large feasts, however, it was impossible for this to happen and all kinds of foods were served together so you could decide what you ate (picture ①).

Medieval chefs liked to flavour the food, partly because then you couldn't taste that it might be well past its 'sell-by' date and would otherwise smell. The sauces they used were often quite thick and flavoured with spices by the handful: ginger, sugar, vinegar, wine, raisins, mace,

cloves, cumin, cardamom, cinnamon, pepper and honey. Colourings were also used: red (sandalwood), yellow (saffron), green (mint or parsley juice), black (burnt bread crumbs). As a result, rich people ate food that was a combination of sweet and acidic flavours (some people have likened it to modern Indian food).

A starter was often a sugar or honey coated sweet made with ginger, anise, cumin, fennel and caraway. After that you would eat fruit, then vegetables such as cabbage, carrots and lettuce, or you might consider them common because they were eaten by the poor. In that case you would go without them. Then you might have a

Entertainment

Most people went to bed early, but from time to time, entertainment would be laid on. These would have included minstrels, jesters and troubadours.

Feasts

When the king visited the castle of one of his subjects, the meals were not just complex, but had to be prepared for vast numbers. When Henry III's daughter was married in 1251, the feast was 1,300 deer, 7,000 hens, 170 boars, 60,000 herring, and 68,500 loaves of bread, To celebrate the enthroning of Archbishop Neville in 1465, 1,000 sheep, 2,000 pigs, 2,000 geese, 4,000 rabbits, and 12 porpoises and seals were eaten.

vegetable and chicken soup, called a **POTAGE**. This might be followed by roasted chicken or lamb, which would be easier to digest than the meat which comes next: beef and pork covered in thick sauces.

The meal ended by drinking spiced wine or eating cheese.

Food presentation was everything. If you had a peacock for dinner, it was skinned, cooked, and then put back in its skin for presentation at the table. Animals were stuffed inside other animals, for example, a pig stuffed with a chicken which would in turn be stuffed with pine nuts. A pike might be boiled at the head, fried in the middle, and roasted at the tail and served with roast eel.

Meals and entertainment for everyone else

So now we have a few bloated rich people slumbering after their huge meal. What was everyone else eating? The main food was bread. Most people were, of necessity, vegetarians for most of the time. When they did get to eat meat it was usually fish. The bread was dipped in potage, which was usually vegetables, but could have a chicken in it on special occasions. The only spices were honey, wine, vinegar and salt. For entertainment, the castle staff might sing songs and tell stories while gathered around a fire in the bailey.

The garrison

The castle was home to a garrison. The garrison was partly made up of men-at-arms, who used pikes, fired arrows and wielded swords, and partly of a number of cavalry soldiers. At times of need, the lord would call on his lesser lords, called KNIGHTS, to come to his aid.

Castles were not home to thousands of armed men. No one could afford the cost. Most castles had a few tens of cavalry and perhaps a few more men-at-arms. Imagine the cavalry troop in the American Wild West forts and you get the idea of the normal scale of things.

A few battles were fought between thousands. Such armies were made up by taking a few dozen from the garrison in each castle along the marching route and by commanding peasants on each estate to leave their fields and join the army.

Although the castle might not have a large garrison, the garrison was vital and it had to have trusted soldiers. Part of this trust was developed through a code of conduct, especially by the knighted cavalry. It was called CHIVALRY.

Cavalry and chevaliers

When the Normans arrived in England they already knew about cavalry and chivalry, for the terms came from France. The French word for knight is chevalier (person skilled in the ways of a horse, after the French word 'cheval').

There were two kinds of mounted soldier. There were the cavalrymen, who were mounted soldiers paid by the lord. They

▶ ① Chain mail used to protect face and neck.

were lightly armoured, but this would be good enough for most purposes. Then there were the knights, who were much more heavily armoured and used only in times of great need (pictures ①, ②, ③ and ④).

Knights were landowners and part of the nobility. They developed a set of rules that involved service, courage and especially a code of honour; a set of manners for medieval fighting gentlemen.

Up for ransom

Being a knight in battle had some advantages. The codes of conduct meant that, if you were taken prisoner you were looked after well while someone went to find the money to ransom you.

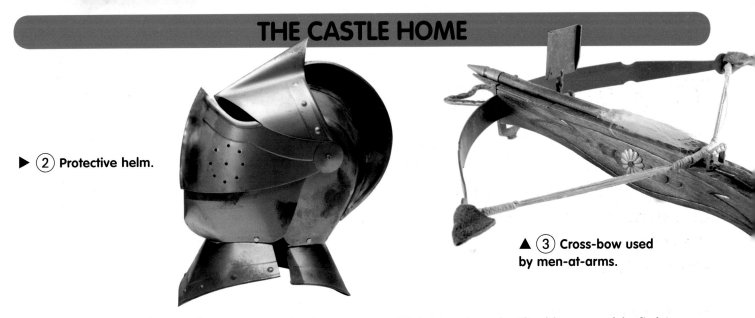

► ② **Protective helm.**

▲ ③ **Cross-bow used by men-at-arms.**

If you were a simple cavalryman, or a foot soldier, you would simply be slaughtered, as no code of chivalry applied to you and you were not going to be worth ransoming either.

Code of conduct

Many of the rules and ways of behaving were copied from the Romans, who the knights saw as glorious soldiers.

Knights also glorified honourable fighters from the Arab world. Even during the Crusades, when Christian knights went off on holy wars to Jerusalem, they recognised the Muslim leader Saladin as a chivalrous knight. Furthermore, many Arab knights had additional skills of being able to read and write and to know how to speak well in company.

Being a knight often meant being clad from head to toe in armour. So how were these knights to identify themselves? If they did brave deeds how were others to recognise that? The medieval way of advertising was to have a coat of arms and other coloured markings.

The knight was originally a riding servant of the king. However, over the centuries, the church influence meant that knights eventually had a code which protected the weak (especially fair maidens) and churches, as well as the Christian religion.

◄ ④ **Reconstruction fight with long, two-handed swords that could be used for slashing down on footsoldiers and also in hand-to-hand fighting, after the horsemen had dismounted.**

Tournaments and jousting

The knights lived by a set of strict rules. These were called chivalry. Nobles were warriors and to keep themselves fit and well-practised, they took part in regular sporting events, but these – tournaments – were wild and uncontrollable. Later they were calmed down to jousting and other individual competitions.

The tournament

In early medieval times, the place where knights showed off their skill was at the tournament (pictures ① and ③). It was another idea borrowed from the Romans, in this case from the chariot races and military exercises between the cavalry in Roman legions.

The mock battle was the centrepiece of the tournament. Two sides battled it out by means of a horseback charge using lances held level (picture ②). The idea was to knock someone off their horse, ride on, turn and ride back (hence tournament, meaning turning around) into the fight to knock another opponent off their horse. There was also jousting, where two knights rode at each other with the aim of dislodging the opponent. However, this was a side-show compared to the battle – called the melée.

The tournament usually ended with both sides being exhausted. The patron of the day would offer lavish banquets and entertainments. Prizes were offered to the best knight on either side (a medieval 'man of the match'), and awarded during the meals.

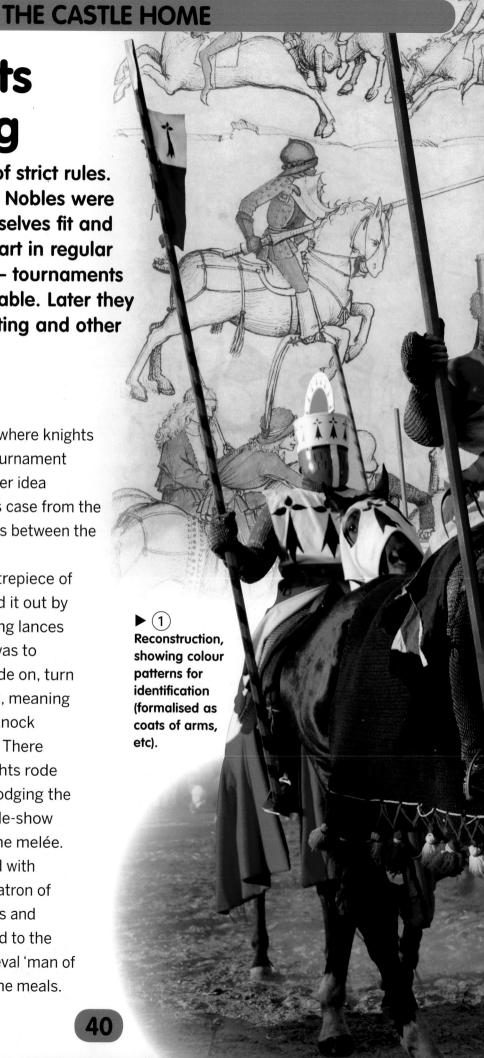

► ①
Reconstruction, showing colour patterns for identification (formalised as coats of arms, etc).

◀ ② A tournament
as shown in a
medieval book.

▼ ③ Reconstruction
of jousting.

Tournaments led to loutish behaviour and kings banned them, or restricted them to certain places (wherever a lord could afford to pay the licence fee!), so they were not found near to every castle. Knights might have to travel a long way to one of the tournament sites.

Early knights wore rings of iron meshed together (**CHAIN MAIL**) (page 38) and a large helmet (a **HELM**) (page 39), but gradually fashion changed to plate armour which was often so heavy the rider had to be lifted up on his horse with the help of his squire. The horse also had to be able to take this weight and so cavalry horses were more like cart horses. Lances for jousting were made of solid oak. They could cause bruising, but could not go through the armour, so deaths were not common. Horses did not gallop (and probably could not under such a weight), but simply ambled, so there was time for the riders to plan their thrust. The same applied to a real battle, when long, slashing swords were mostly used instead of a lance (see page 39). Knights did not run full pelt at the opponent, for that increased the chances of missing the target.

Domesday

Castles were the centrepiece of medieval life, which began with the conquest by William of Normandy. We know exactly what life was like in Norman times because William had one of the world's most famous books written about it. It is called the Domesday Book.

England covers an area of 130,000 sq km. But beyond this fact, William had a problem. He did not know how it was used or who owned it. If William was to raise the money he needed as tax, then he had to have some reliable and reasonably fair way of knowing what each person could afford. The Saxons (who ruled before him) had not got up-to-date records for the whole country, so William could not just pick up a set of books and get to work calculating tax. He had to get the book made in the first place. This is why, not long after he took over, he commissioned the recording of the land of England, who lived on it, who owned it, what they did with it, how much it was worth and so on. He also wanted to know how much tax had been paid to the Saxon kings before him. This great work, when put together, was called the Domesday Book (pictures ① and ②).

The Domesday Book

The name Domesday comes from the Old English word dom, which means reckoning. So domesday means 'the day of reckoning'.

It was an enormous survey, completed in 1086. It was written in a kind of shorthand Latin. When the Normans arrived, less than a quarter (30,000 sq

km) had been cultivated. Today about 60,000 sq km are cultivated, so about half of all land had been used, or, looked at the other way, half of the land remained to be cultivated and was mostly still woodland and open pasture.

Some of it was described as wasteland. Much of this was on the borders with Wales, and possibly Scotland, which could not be used because of border raids. Other land was 'laid to waste' changing it from farmland to provide hunting areas for the king. These were often called forests but they were not necessarily wooded (for example, the New Forest, Hampshire).

▶ ② **Translated extract from the Domesday Book.**

▼ ① **The Domesday Book.**

Ely is assessed as 10 hides. There is land for 20 ploughs. In demesne [are] 5 hides, and there can be a sixth.

There are 40 villains, each [with] 15 acres, with 14 ploughs.

There are 28 cottars and 20 slaves.

From the fisheries, 3,750 eels, [and] from gifts [of fish], 2s3d. [There is] meadow for 20 ploughs, [and] pastures for the livestock of the vill. There are 3 arpents of vineyards.

In all it is worth £30; when received, £20; TRE £33.

All this manor always was and is demesne.

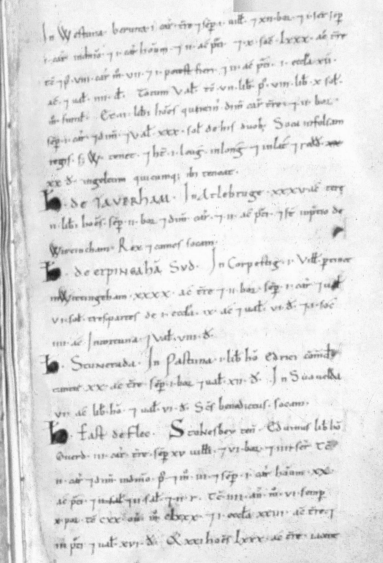

Life in Norman times

If you think that we live in a country full of class divisions, that is nothing compared to the Norman times, when people not only knew their place, they were very firmly put and kept in their place by the feudal system. Some English people of the time were even slaves.

The Saxons had lords, knights, farmers and slaves. The Normans continued this system and it became known as the **FEUDAL SYSTEM**.

The feudal system

The feudal system grouped people into categories in which everyone knew their place. It had three basic parts:

(i)   The serf, free peasant or slave, who worked for all;

(ii) the lord (king, knight or baron) who protected the people and therefore who fought for all; and

(iii) the church, which protected souls and therefore prayed for all.

Of course, there were very few knights, barons and clergy. Nearly everyone was a peasant and near the bottom of the pile.

Life was relatively comfortable for the few, but for the many it was hard and short. People were poor and most did not have a change of clothes. It was not common to wash clothes, or indeed yourself, in these times. Poor people might live to their 30s, but it was uncommon even for the rich to live beyond their 50s.

At the top of this system was the king. He was the only one who could own land outright. He kept about a fifth of all land for himself directly. All of his barons were allotted land by the king which, in theory, remained the king's land, although they could buy and sell it. These were called fiefdoms. The greatest tracts of land were given to the barons who had fought with William. In this way, the twelve leading barons controlled a quarter of England. Few Saxon lords remained, as most had been killed fighting with Harold at Hastings and elsewhere. The barons had to pay the king taxes and promise to provide knights if the king needed to raise an army. Lords also had to pay to build castles. A quarter of the country was also given to the Catholic Church, which had given the invasion its blessing. It was given to them forever but they were not allowed to sell it.

These great areas of land were divided up into smaller units run by lesser lords – knights who got the land on condition that they would serve their lord in times of trouble. The areas they owned were called manors.

The land in a manor was divided into strips which the lord's tenants farmed. These areas of farmland were called open fields. Two fields were always under the plough and one always in fallow. The idea was that the land needed to rest periodically in order to gets its fertility back after being used for crops.

Just like the king, the lords needed money to run their estates and they got this partly by renting out land to peasants. The lord could also raise taxes from market stalls in towns. It was a great incentive for setting up new towns, and huge numbers of Charter Towns, as they were called, were built in early medieval times. The name comes from the fact that the king had to approve (and be paid for) setting up a new town and issuing a charter (a kind of permit). Many of these towns survive.

The church did not pay for its parish priests. Priests who worked in parish churches were paid by the tithes (a tax of one tenth of earnings) paid by their congregations.

William I needed churchmen because they were, in general, the only ones who could read and write and so help him to administer the kingdom.

Soon after the conquest, large numbers of monks arrived to live on the lands they had been granted. They founded new abbeys and used local people to build them and to work for them. As a result abbey and town often had close ties.

Abbeys were usually built on new land in the countryside, but sometimes they were built close to towns.

Replanning the countryside

In Saxon times villages had been loose collections of houses close to the fields they worked. But during medieval times many were replanned and rebuilt by agreement between lord and peasants, and this was the time when features like a large green (for keeping livestock), a fish pond and sometimes even a church were first built. This is why, for example, many churches date from Norman times.

Glossary

BAILEY The area inside the curtain wall.

BURGAGE PLOT A long narrow strip of town land rented to a freeman by the lord of the manor. The narrow end faced the street.

CASTLE A fortified home of a medieval nobleman or king.

CHAIN MAIL Flexible armour made of iron links. A shirt made from mail is a hauberk.

CHIVALRY The way that medieval knights fought to a set of well-defined rules.

CRENELLATION The pattern of alternating higher and lower tops to the walls of many medieval castles. Also known as battlements.

CRUSADES A series of religious military campaigns by catholics and whose aim was to regain Christian control of the Holy Land. They occurred between 1095 and 1291.

CRYPT A stone chamber in the lowermost part of a castle.

CURTAIN WALL The main outer wall of the castle.

DRAWBRIDGE A bridge over a moat that could be lifted to stop attackers reaching the castle gate.

FEUDAL SYSTEM The medieval arrangement whereby each part of society had duties to another. Lords had the duty to protect peasants and peasants (through taxes) had a duty to support their lord.

FORT A large area enclosed by a wall designed to hold a garrison.

GARDEROBE A very simple toilet set in a small private room in a castle wall.

GREAT HALL The main living area of the castle owner and the place where business was conducted.

HELM OR HELMET A protective hat designed to prevent injury to the head. It was made of iron.

KEEP The central tower of an early castle.

KNIGHT A lesser nobleman who might have a small fortified house, or live in the court of a king or baron. His main duty was to be part of the heavy cavalry during battle.

MOAT The ditch around a castle used to help protection. Many, but not all, moats had water in.

MOTTE The mound of earth on which the keep was built.

NORMAN People descended from Vikings (Norsemen) and who gave their names to Normandy, in northern France. The Norman kings ruled England between 1066 and 1154.

PEASANT A peasant is a farmer who lives from a small plot of ground and who owes taxes and duties to a lord.

PORTCULLIS A metal grille that could be lowered to block the route through the gatehouse.

POSTERN A small, often hidden, gate in a curtain wall designed to allow escape or to allow the garrison to make a surprise attack.

POTAGE A thick soup or stew mostly containing vegetables, and cooked until most of the water has boiled off.

SIEGE A way of attacking a castle by surrounding it and trying to starve the defenders out.

TUDOR A period of English history ruled by the Tudors and beginning with Henry VII in 1485.

WARD The area within the outer walls of a double-walled castle. The area inside the inner wall was the inner ward and the area between the walls was the outer ward.

Index

abbey 46
archers 10, 23, 24
armour 38–39, 41

bailey 6, 8, 9, 12–13, 23, 25, 37, 47
baron 24, 45–46
battering ram 10, 23, 24
battlement
    see crenellation
belfry 22, 23
burgage plot 20, 47
burgh 4

Caernarfon castle 14–15
Caerphilly castle 14–15, 27
Cardiff castle 5, 8
castle 4 *and throughout*, 47
cavalry 5, 10, 13, 38–41
chain mail 38, 41, 47
chapel 5, 6, 9, 13, 17
Charter Town 46
chivalry 38–39, 40, 47
church 24, 39, 45–46
coat of arms 39
constable 22, 23, 35
crenellation 6, 10, 11, 14, 47
Crusades 5, 39, 47
crypt 9, 47
curtain wall 5, 6, 8, 9, 10, 15, 17, 24, 30, 47

drawbridge 6, 9, 10, 11, 47
Domesday 42–43
dungeon 9

entertainment 34, 37, 40–41

feast 36–37
feudal system 45, 47
fiefdom 46
food 36–37

fort 4, 47

garderobe 32, 33, 47
garrison 9, 12, 18, 22. 38–39
gatehouse 6, 10, 11, 13, 23
great hall 5, 9, 13, 27, 28–29, 31, 32, 34–35, 47

Harlech castle 11
helm 39, 41, 47

Iron Age 4, 8

joust 5, 40–41

keep 5, 6, 8, 9, 13, 16, 24–25, 28–29, 31, 34, 47
kitchen 32, 36–37
knight 10, 38–41, 45, 46, 47

loo
    see garderobe

Magna Carter 24
manor 46
medieval 12, 20, 21, 36–37, 39, 40–41, 42–43, 46
moat 5, 6, 9, 10, 18, 47
motte 4, 5, 6, 8–9, 16, 47
murder hole 11

Norman 5, 16–17, 28, 38, 42–43, 44–46, 47

peasant 4, 12, 38, 45–46, 47
Peveril castle 33
Portchester castle 29
portcullis 6, 10, 11, 30, 47
postern 6, 9, 22, 47
potage 32, 37, 47

ransom 22, 38–39

Rochester castle 24–25, 28–29
Romans 4, 39, 40

Saxons 4, 42, 45
scaling ladder 10, 23
serf 45
siege 22–23, 24–25, 47
siege engine 6, 10, 22, 23, 25
slave 44–45
stairs 11, 30–31

toilet
    see garderobe
tournament 5, 40–41
tower 6, 8–9, 10, 14–15
Tower of London 5, 16–17
treachery 23
Tudors 5, 47

undermining 23, 25

wall *see* curtain wall
ward 6, 12, 14, 47
Warkworth castle 6–7, 9, 11, 12, 18–21, 26
watchtower 6, 9, 15
well 6, 28
Windsor castle 5, 16, 17